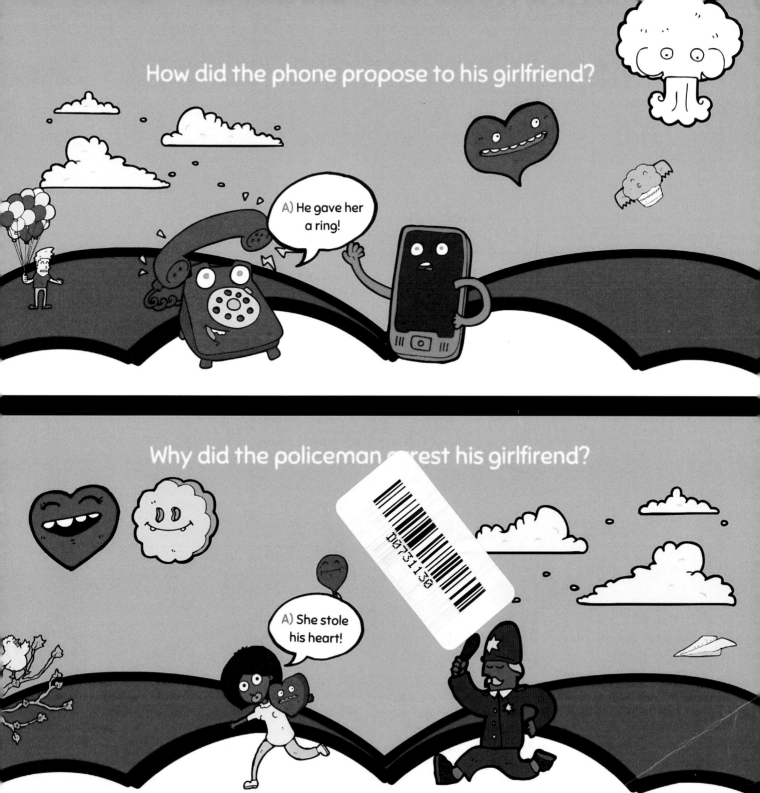

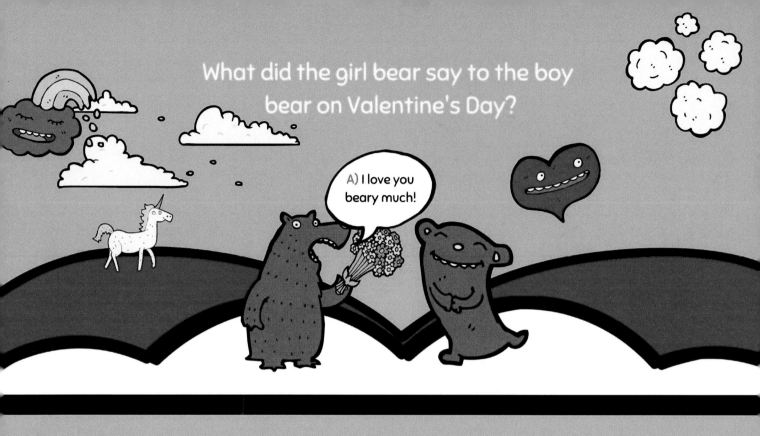

What did the girl bear say to the boy bear on Valentine's Day?

A) I love you beary much!

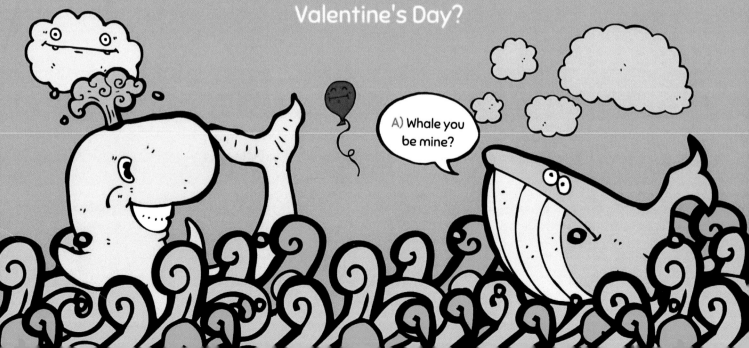

What did the whale say to his sweetheart on Valentine's Day?

A) Whale you be mine?

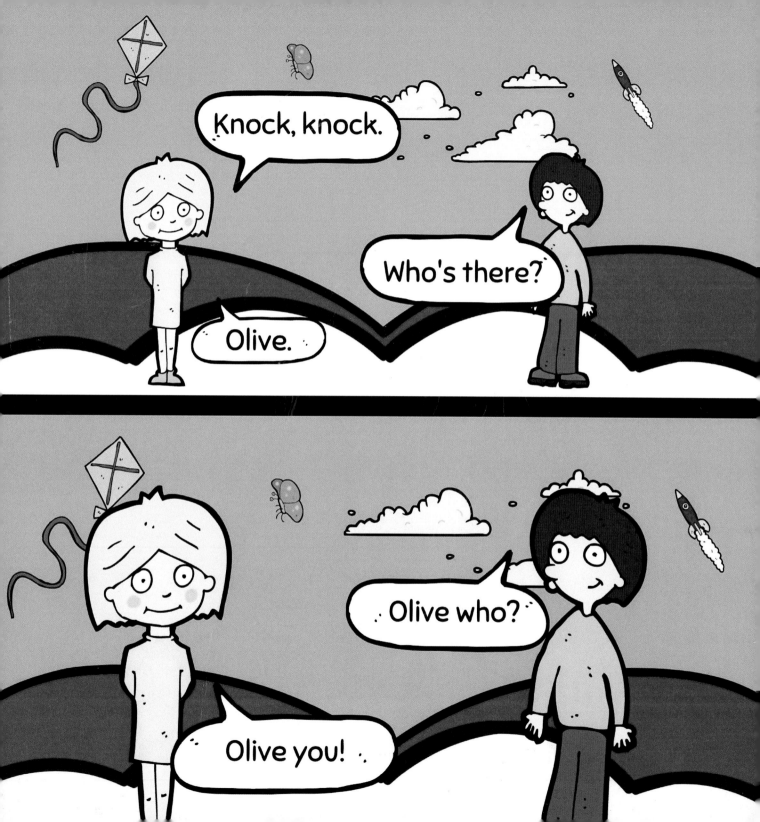

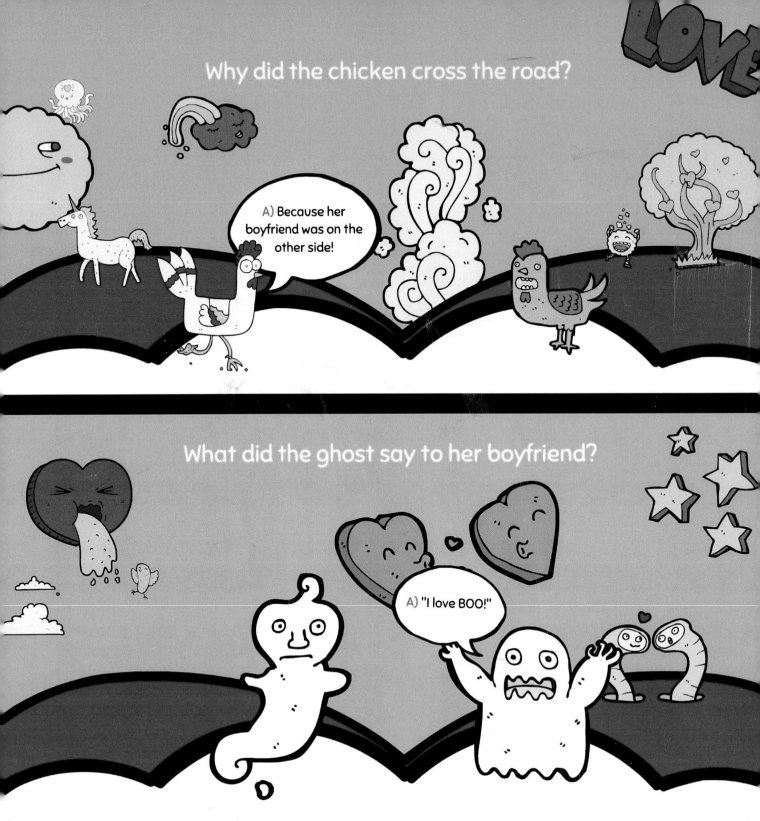

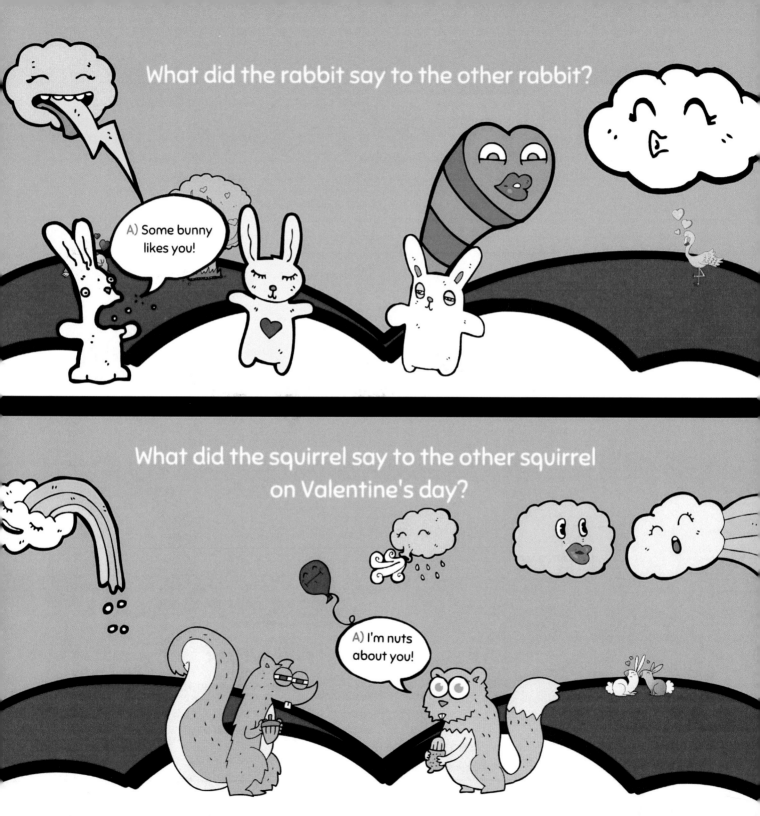

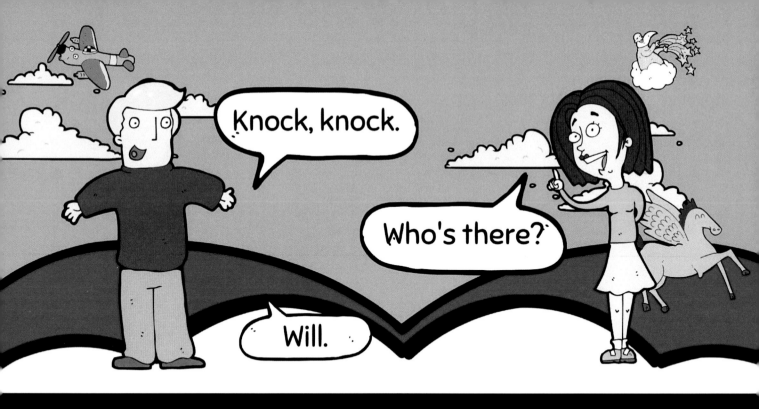
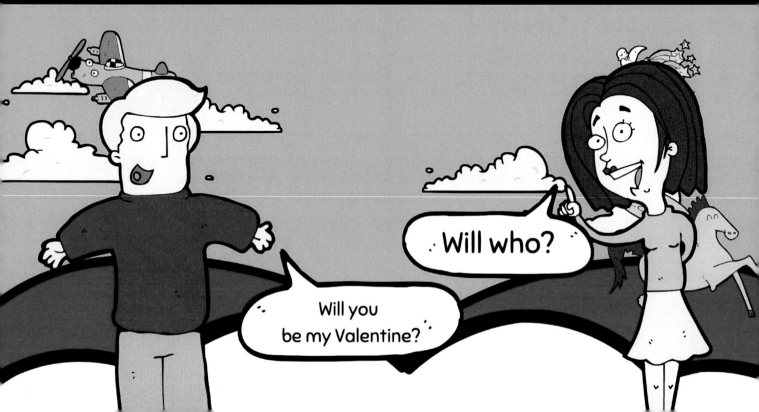

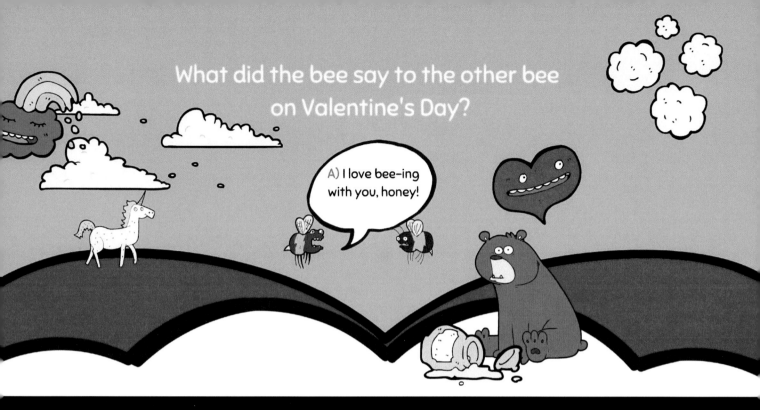

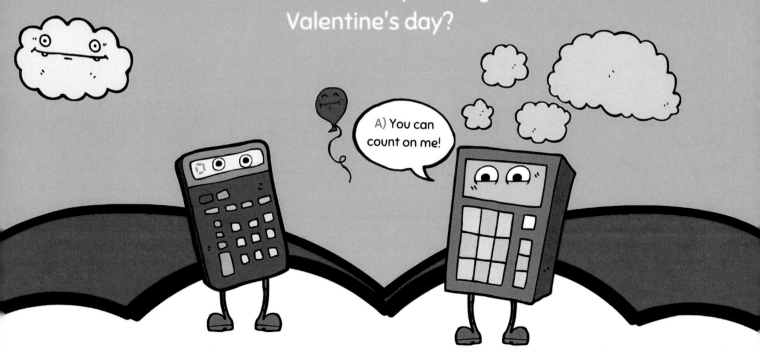

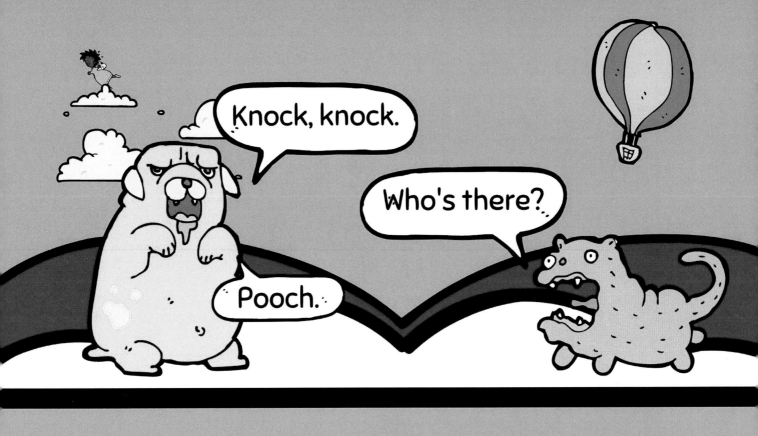

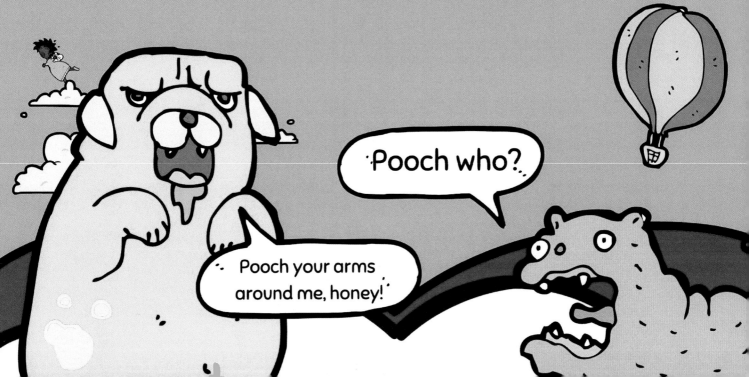

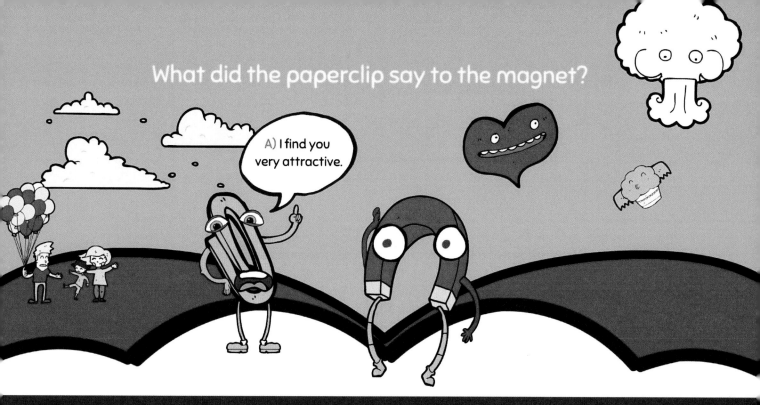

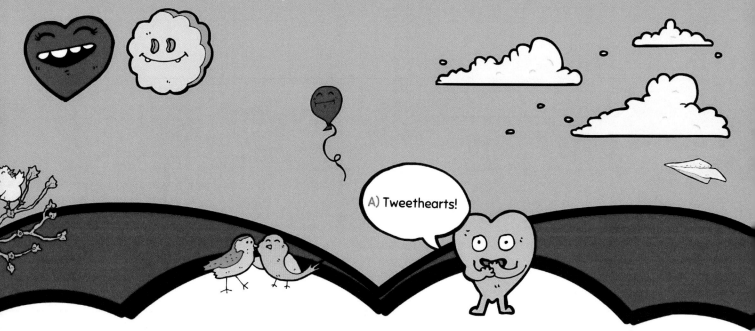

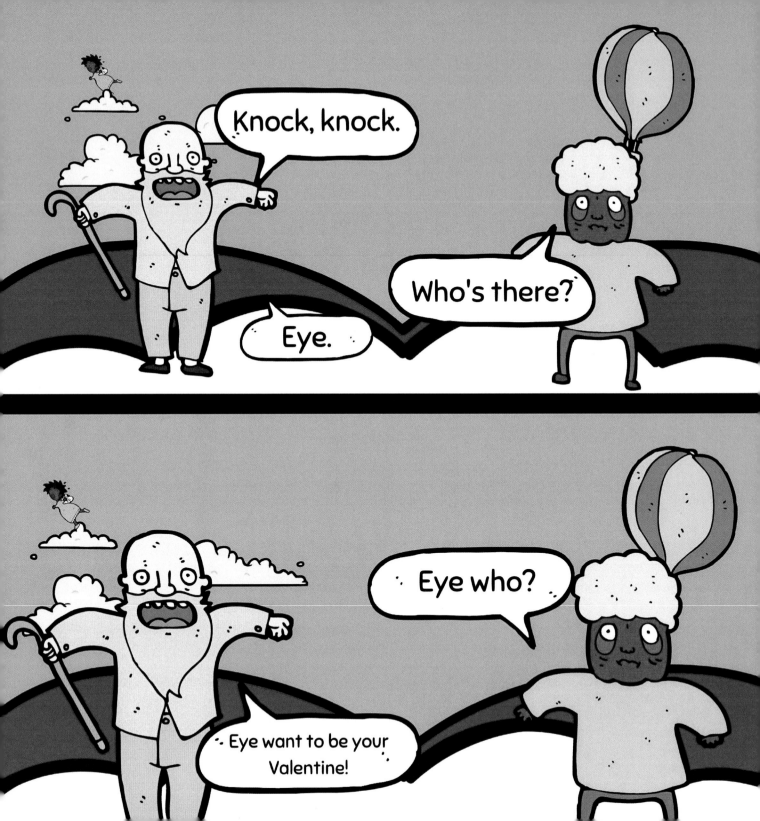

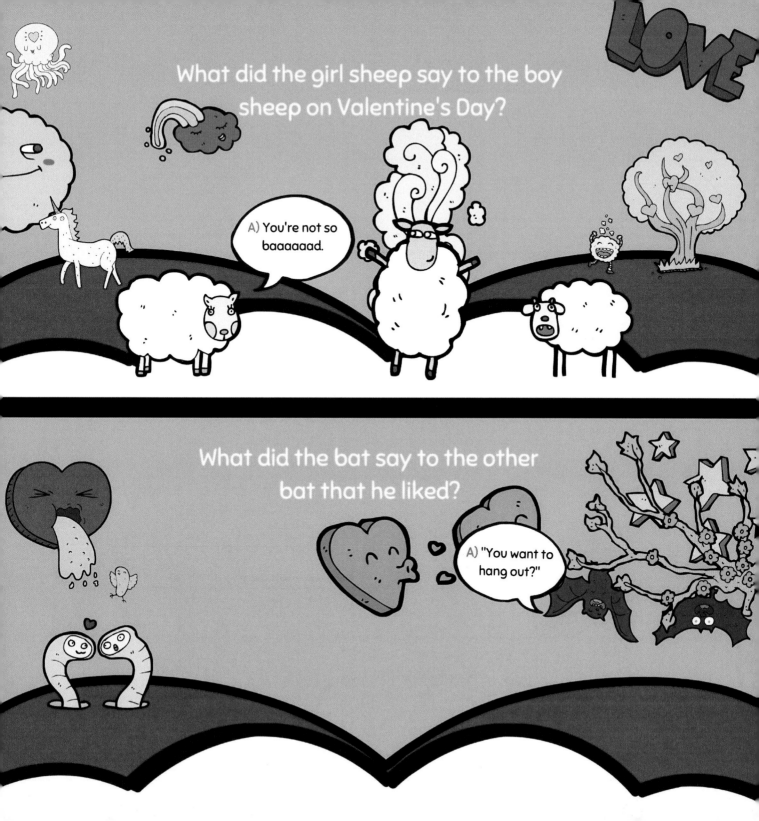

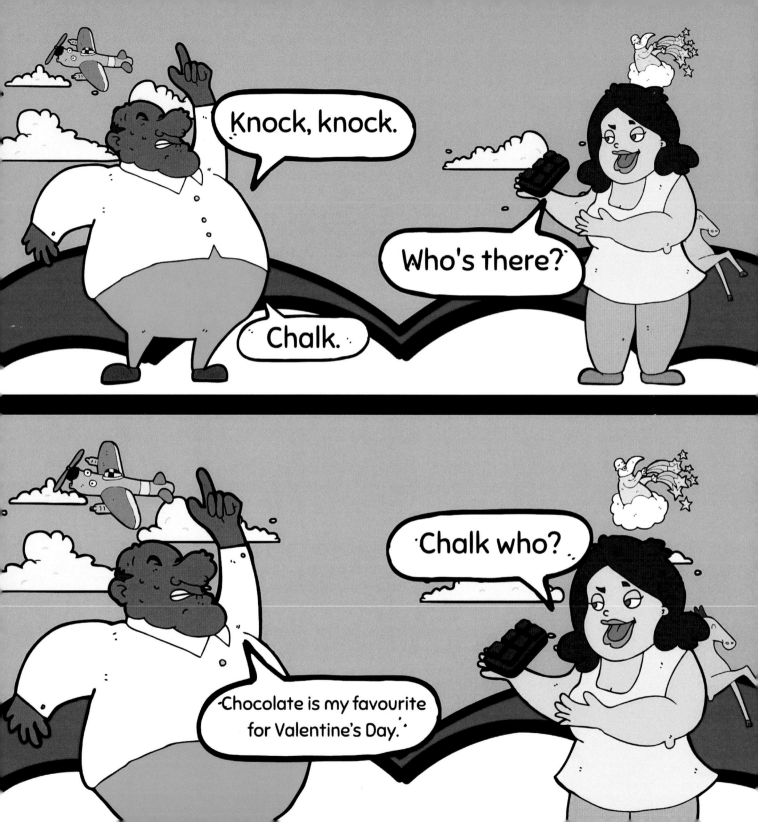

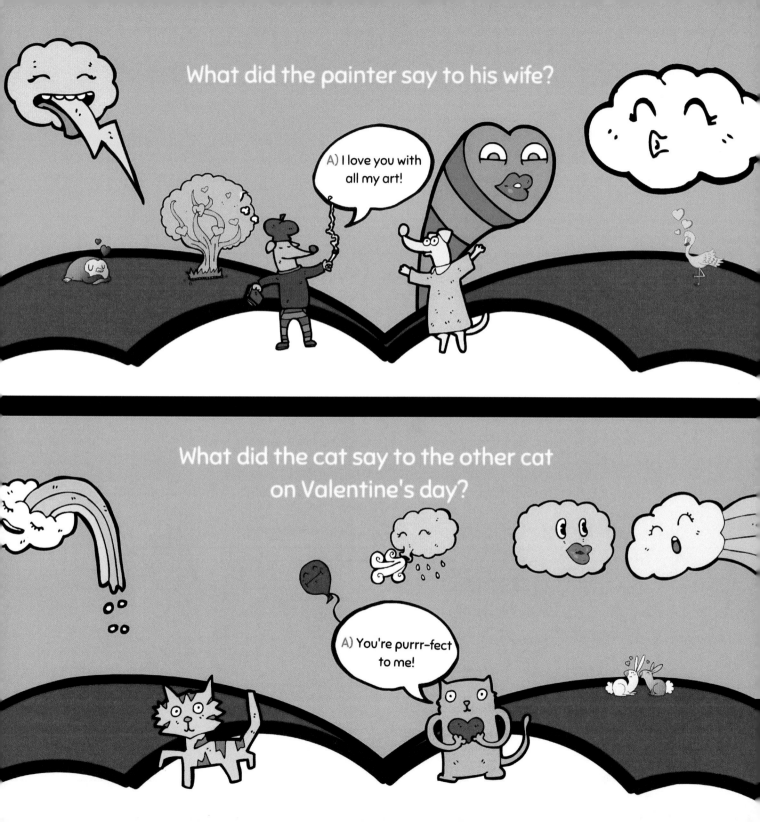

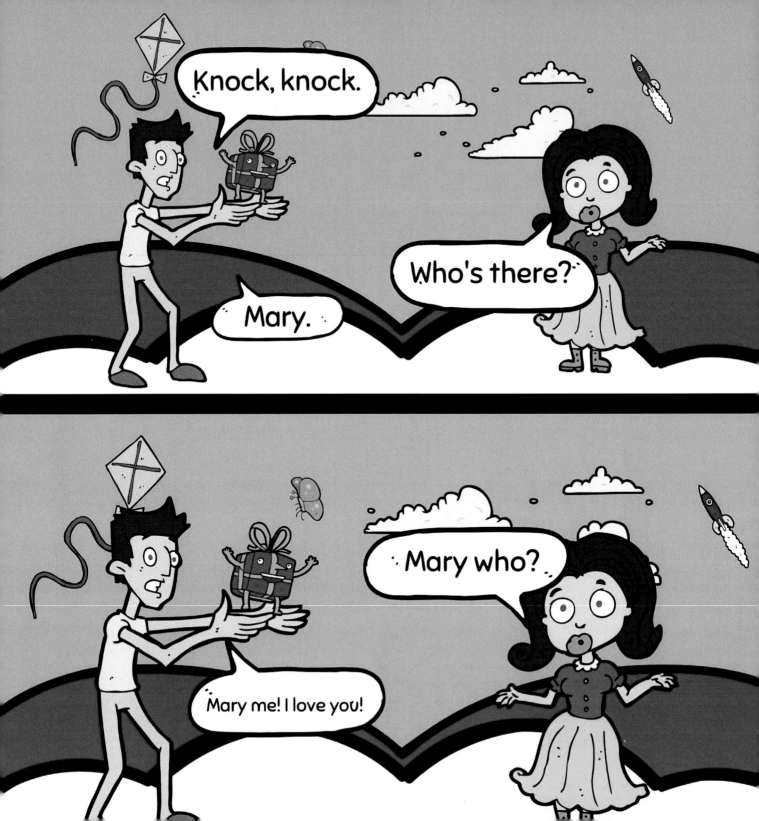

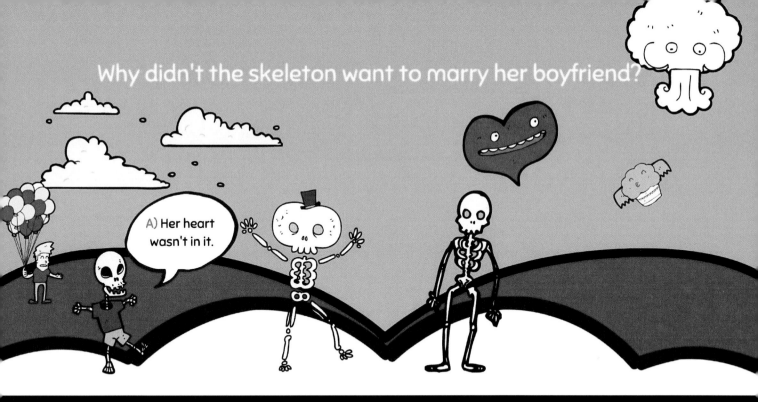

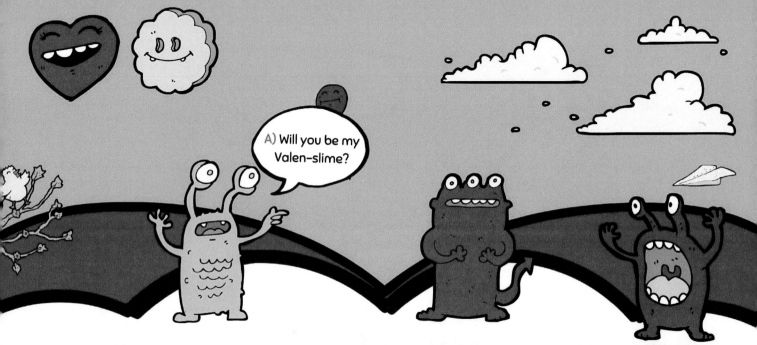

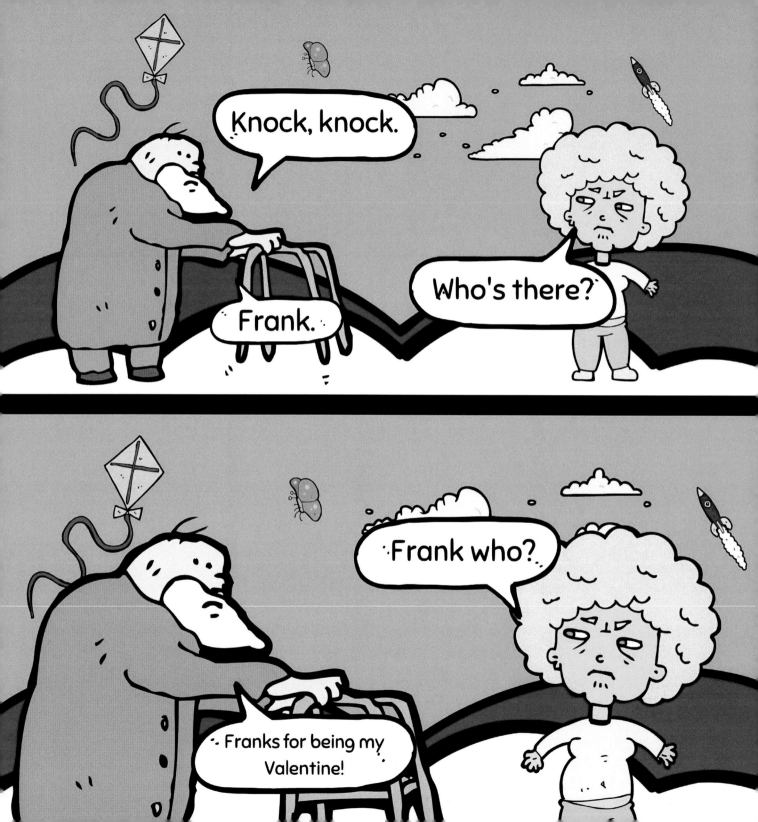

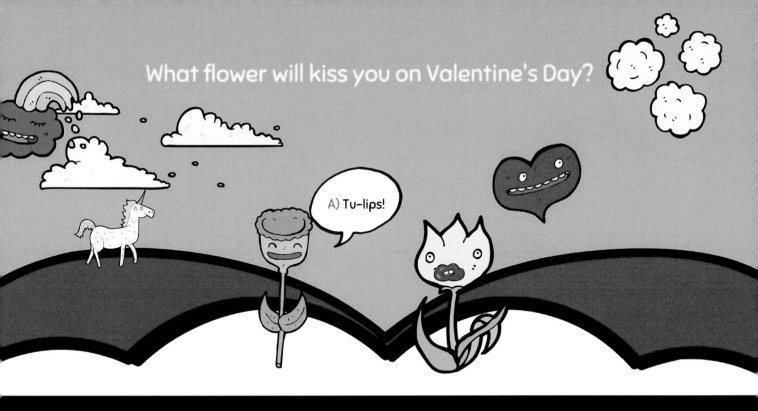

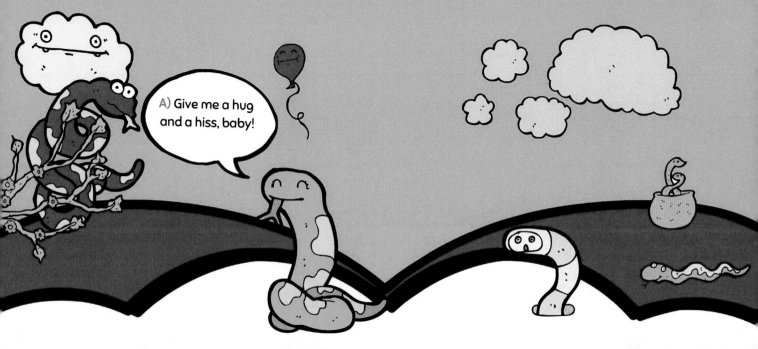

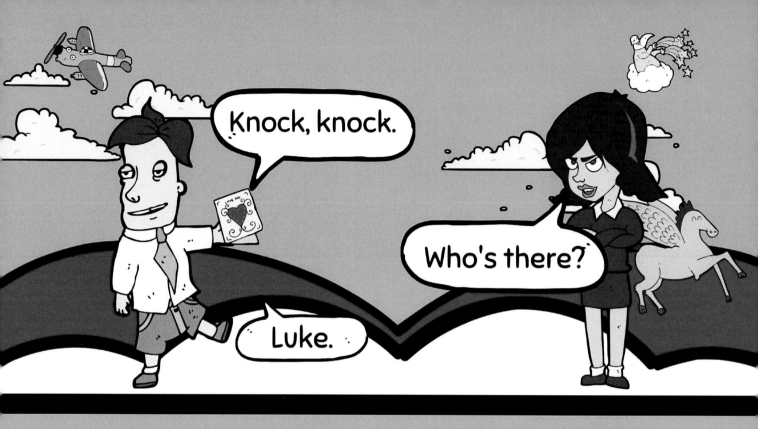

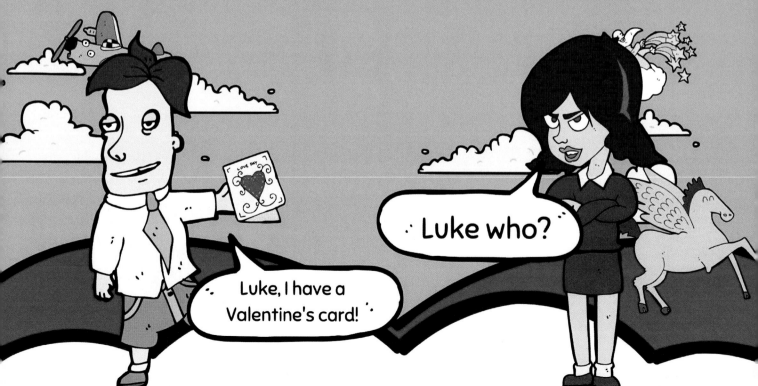

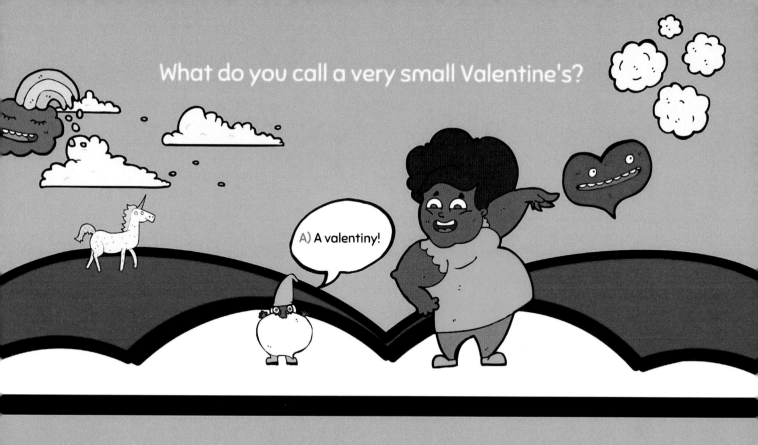

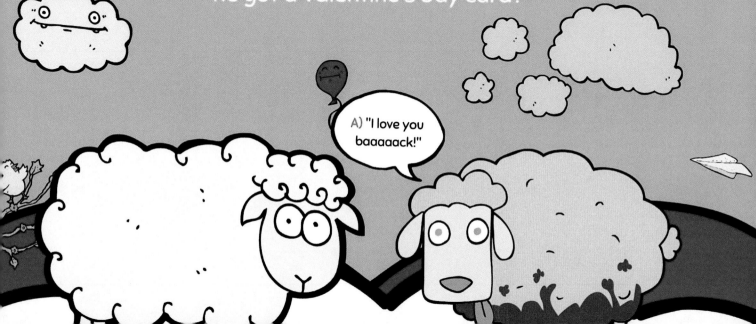

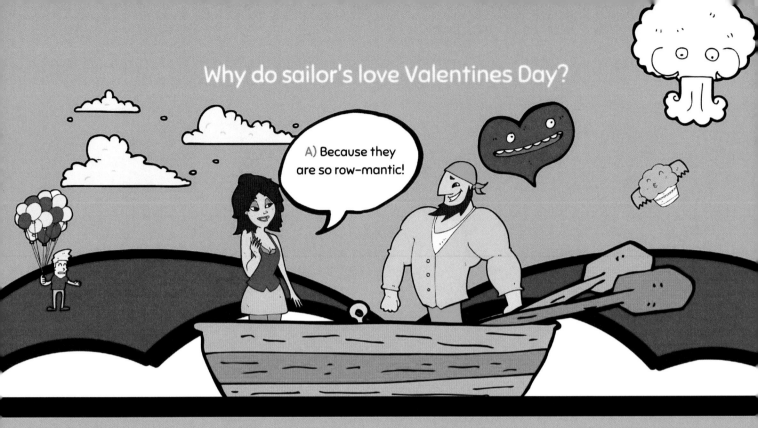

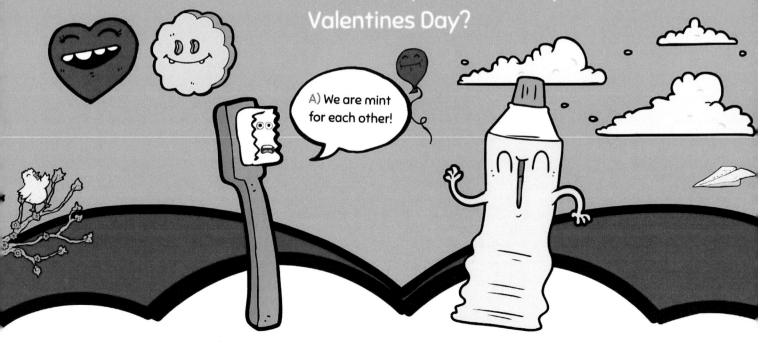

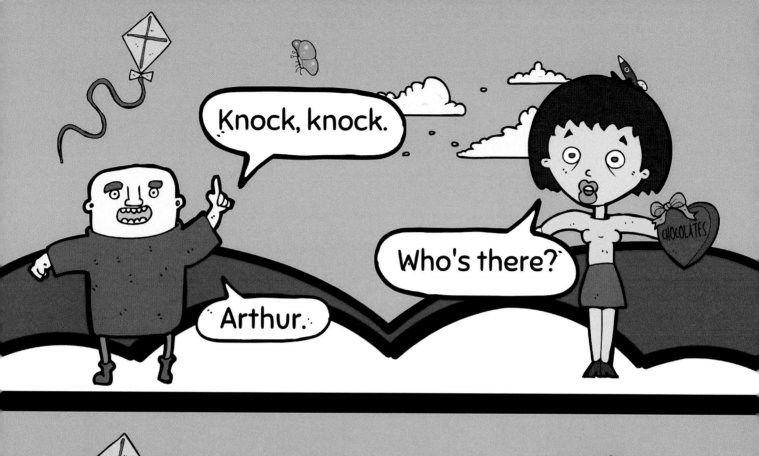
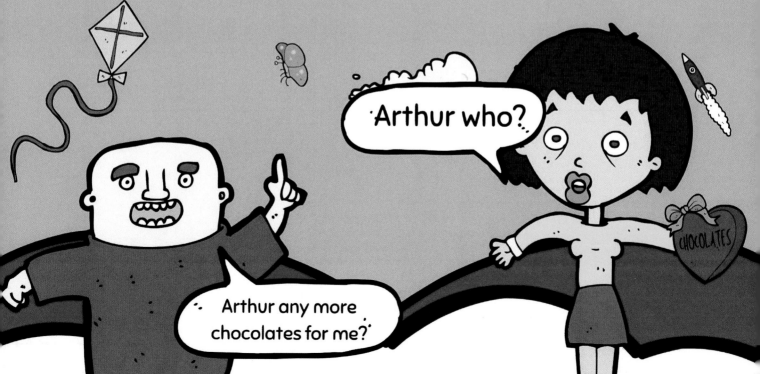

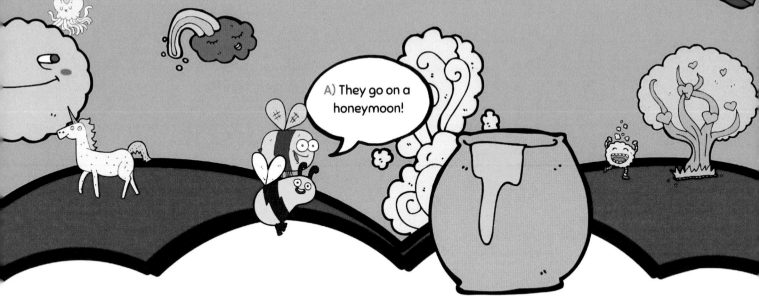

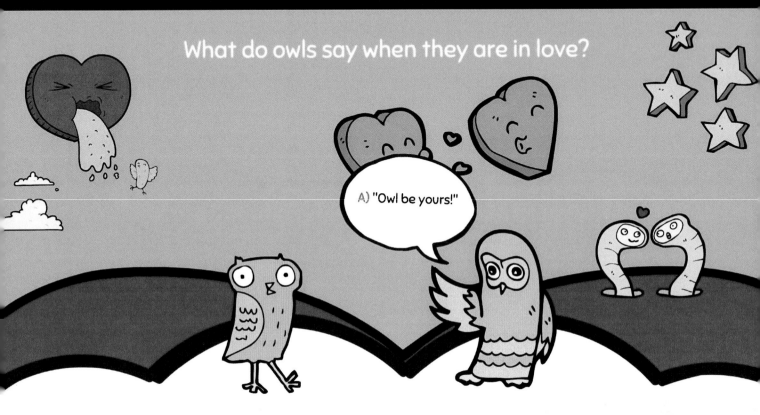

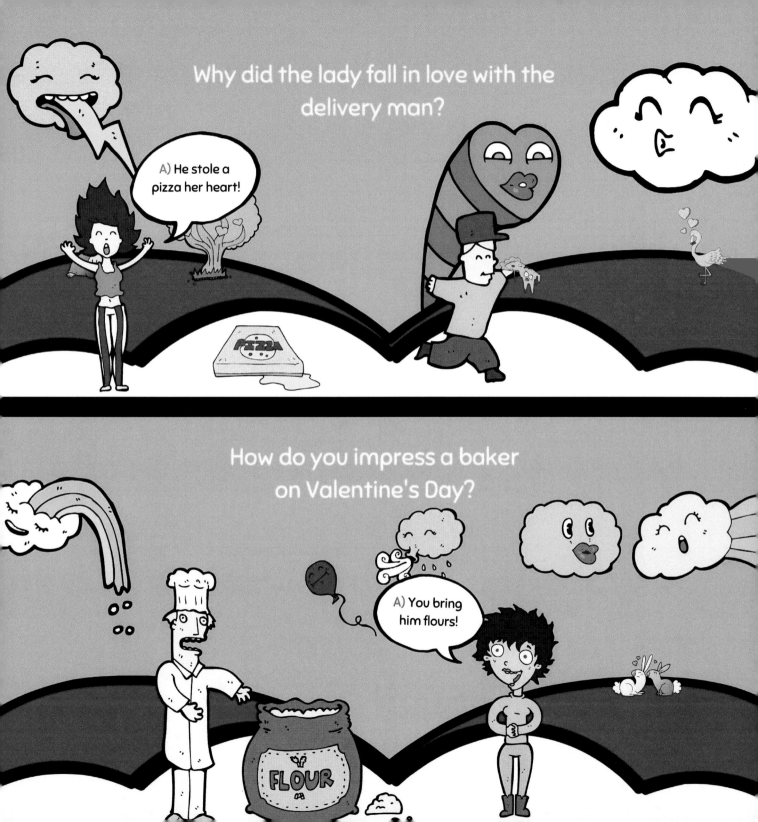

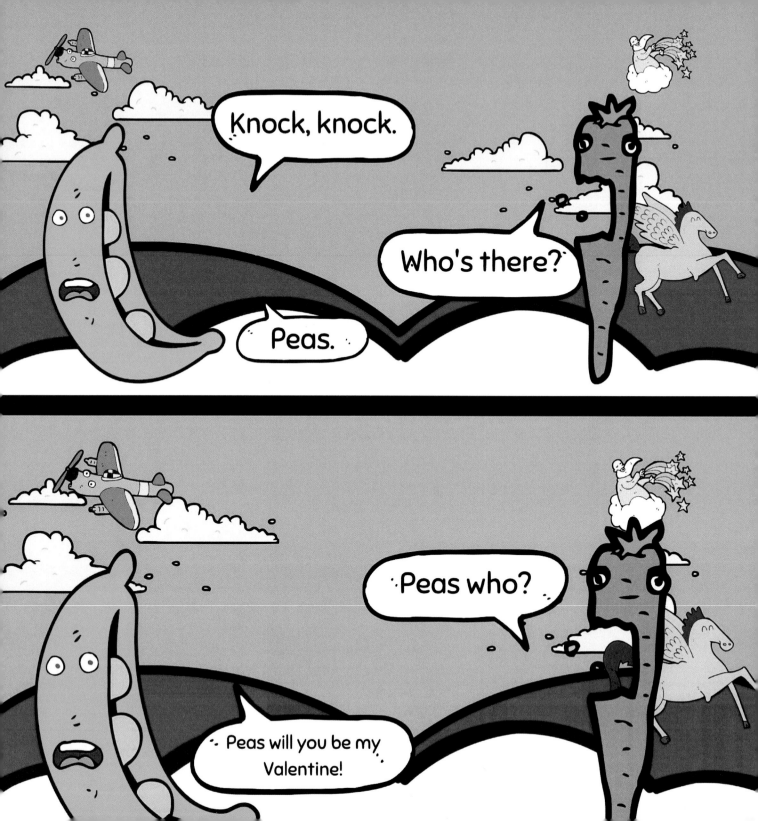

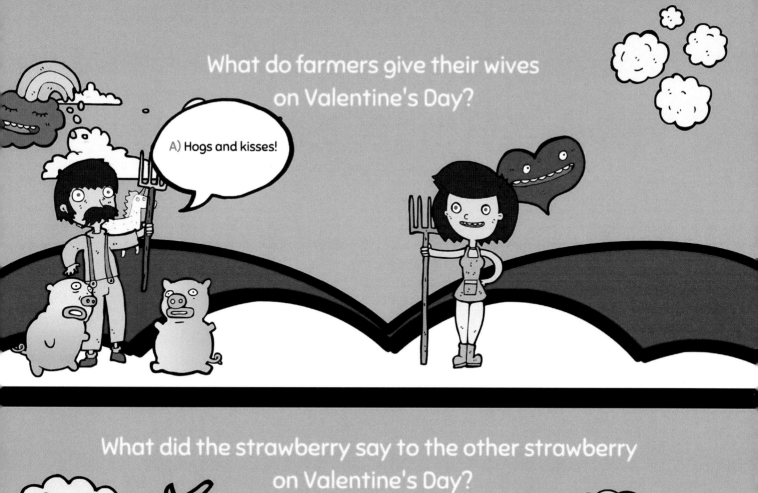

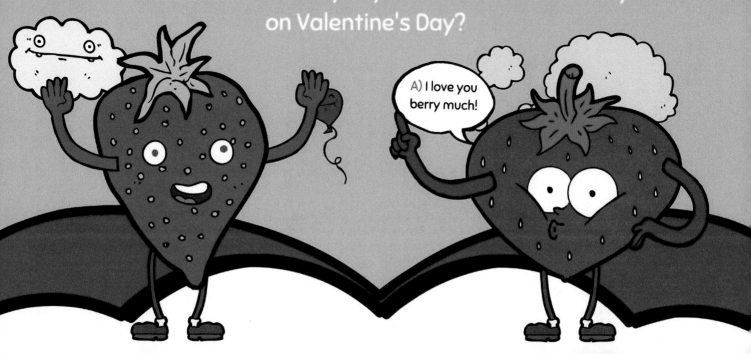

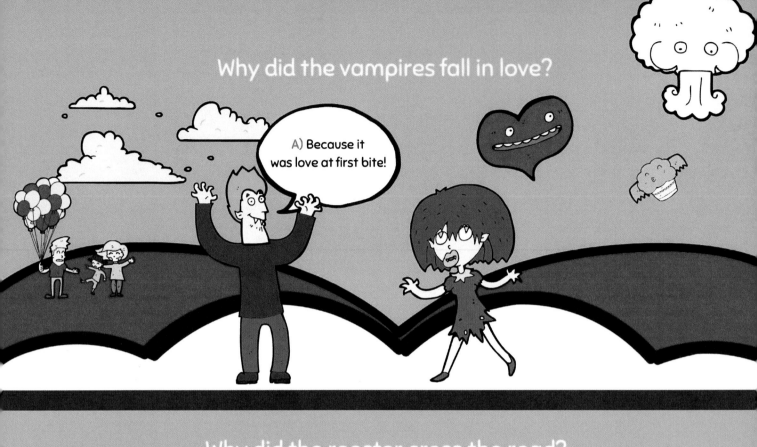

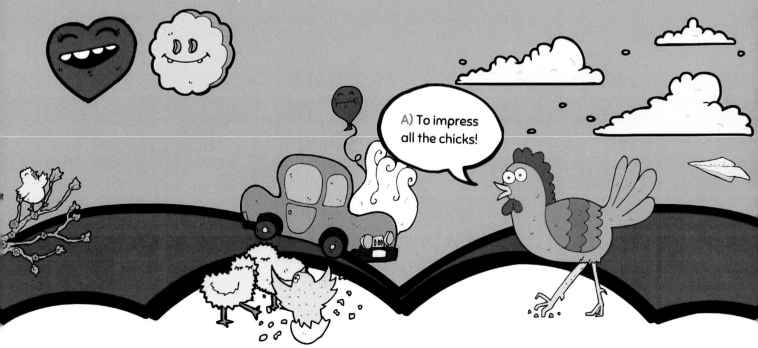

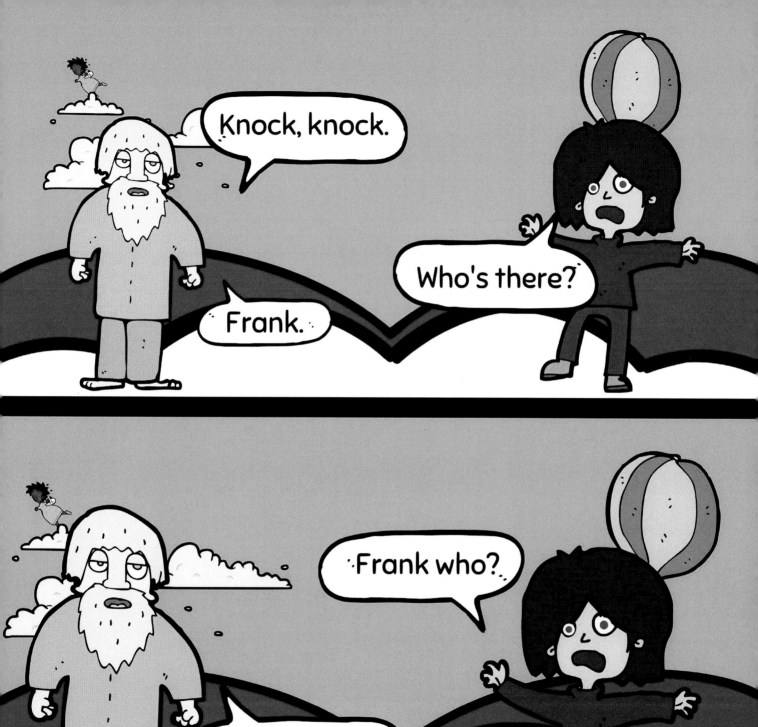

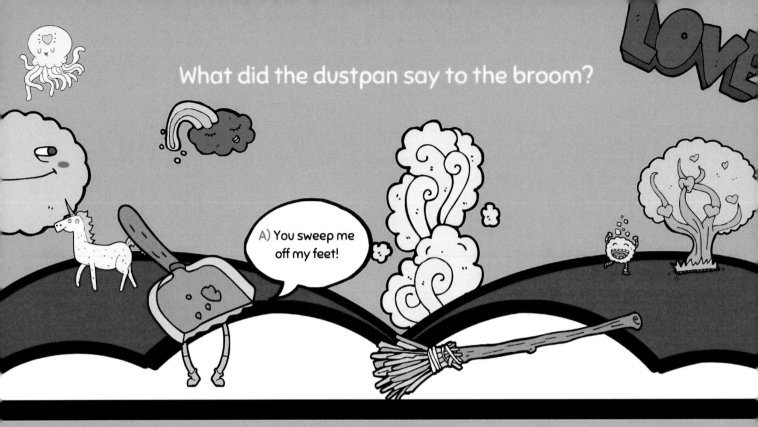

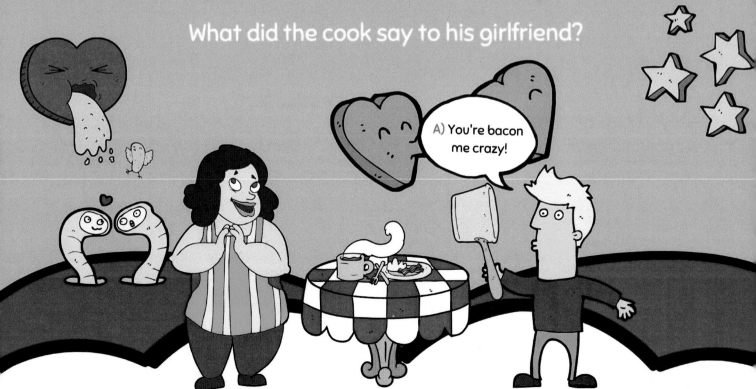

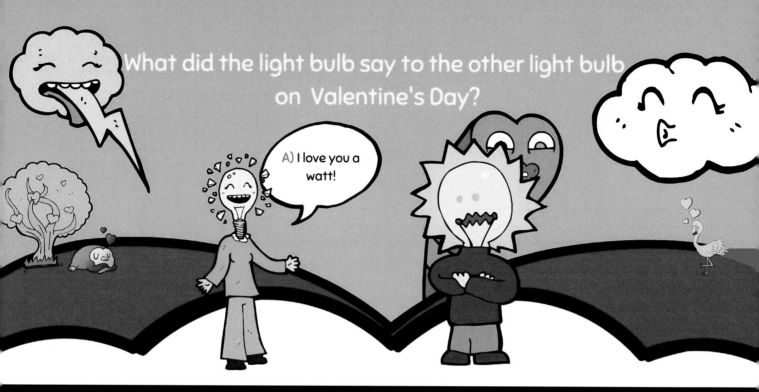

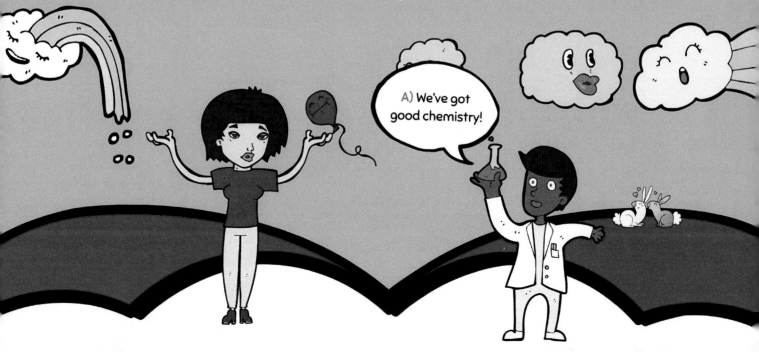

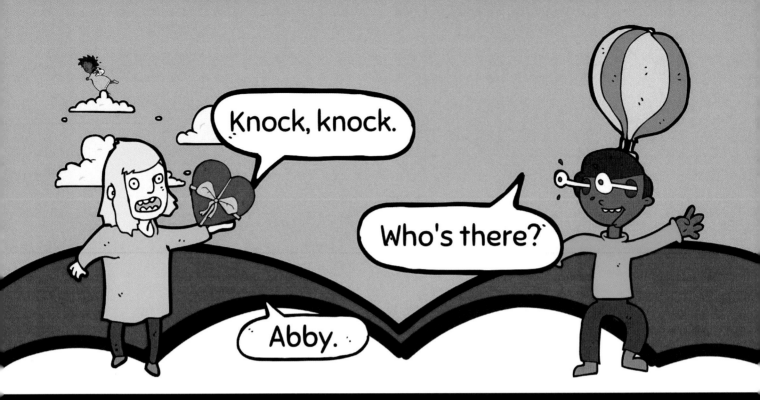
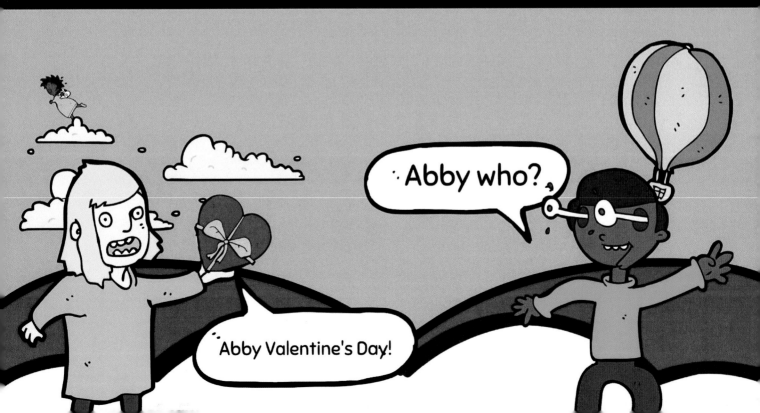

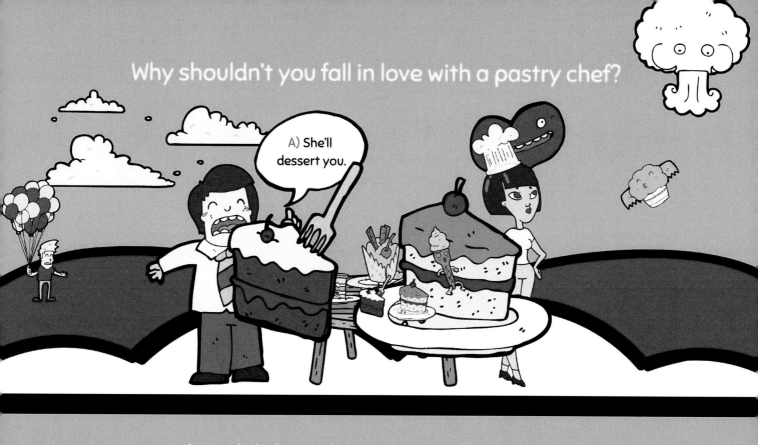

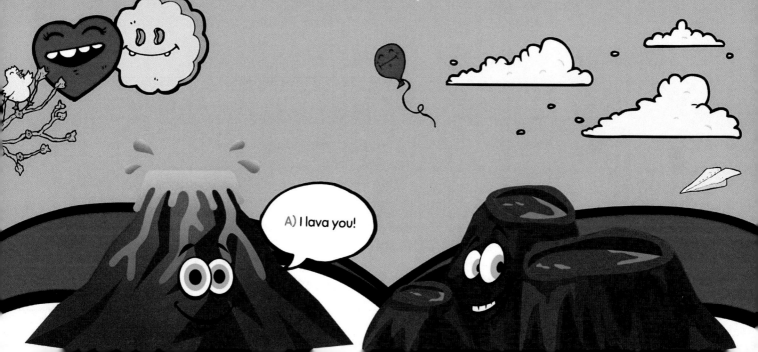

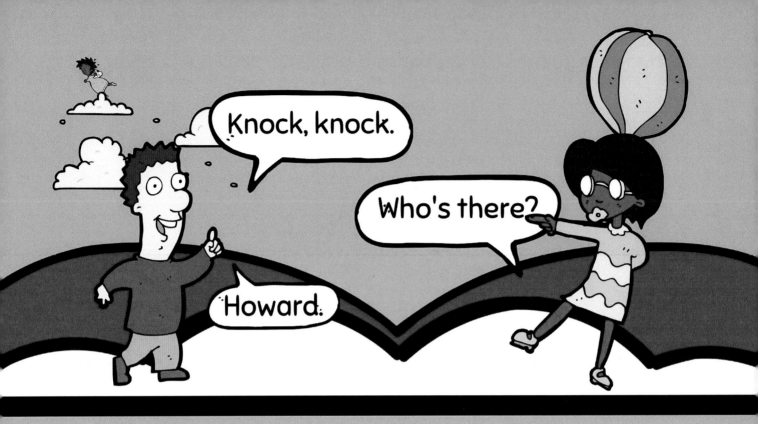
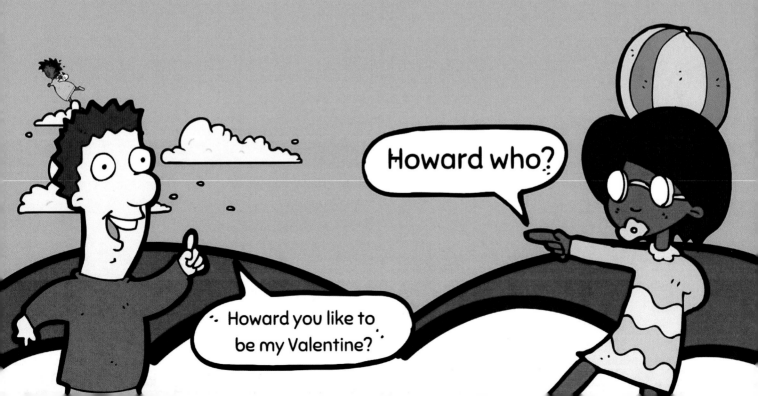

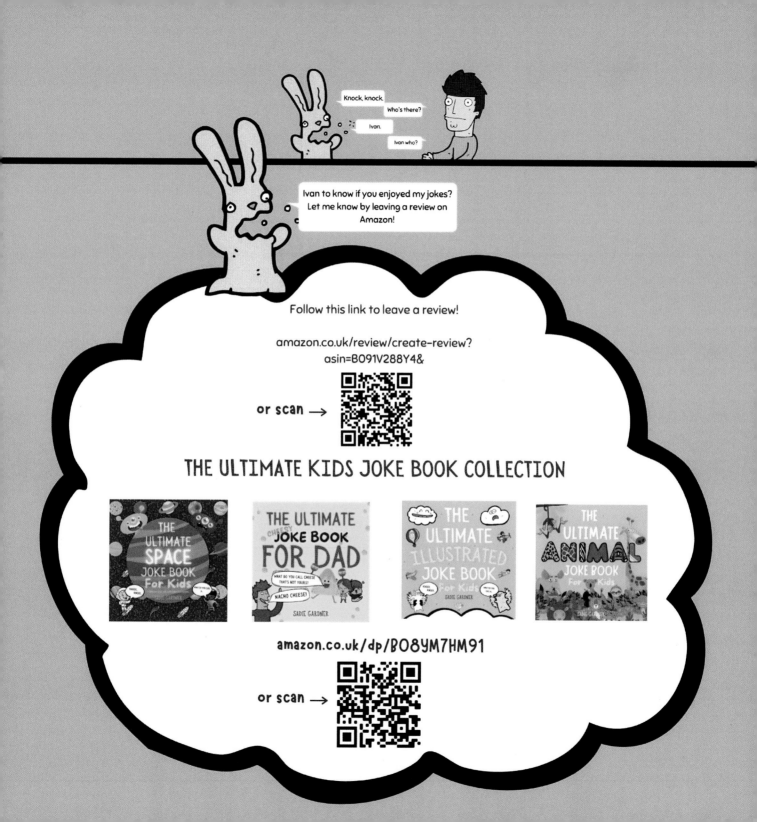

Made in the USA
Las Vegas, NV
09 February 2023

67210352R00021